Boards on Fire!

Boards on Fire!
INSPIRING LEADERS TO
RAISE MONEY JOYFULLY

Susan Howlett

WORD & RABY PUBLISHING
SEATTLE, WASHINGTON

Copyright © 2010 by Susan Howlett
All rights reserved.

Third printing April 2014
ISBN 978-0-9842772-7-8
Library of Congress Control Number
2010934744

Printed in the United States of America
10 09 08 07 06 05 04 03
Word & Raby Publishing, Seattle

Publisher's Cataloging-in-Publication
Howlett, Susan
        Boards on fire : inspiring leaders to
    raise money joyfully / Susan Howlett.
        p. cm.
        LCCN 2010934744
        ISBN-13: 978-0-9842772-7-8
        ISBN-10: 0-9842772-7-7
        1. Fund raising. 2. Nonprofit
    organizations—Finance. 3. Nonprofit
    organizations--Management. 4. Boards
    of directors.   I. Title.
    HG177.H69 2010
    658.15'224
    QBl10-600167

Copies available from:
Word & Raby Publishing
260 NE 43rd Street
Seattle, WA 98105-6549
www.wordandraby.com

Contents

You're Not Alone

You've asked board members to approach others to support your organization, and they say they will (and probably mean to)—but they don't.

You're not alone. Most board members behave the same way.

Countless books, videos, workshops, and conference breakouts have been devoted to getting boards to raise money, but they focus on tactics and rational solutions.

What they don't address is the **deep-seated resistance** board members feel when they're put in the position of asking.

This book will help you understand the sources of their resistance and what **you** can do to remove the barriers that keep them from raising money joyfully.

Whether you're the executive director, development director, board president, chair of the fundraising committee, or a consultant, you can help your colleagues look at the systemic patterns that keep leaders from igniting their passion.

Thankfully, you already hold the answers found within these pages, in your mind and your heart: they're just arranged differently. I trust that by seeing the solutions in this light, you'll be able to foster happier, more engaged boards who experience joy and satisfaction in fundraising.

Jumping In: Leaders Know When They're Not Safe

When my kids were preschoolers, we took them to the neighborhood pool for swimming lessons. The first night, I was intrigued by a mother at the side of the pool who could NOT get her three-year-old into the water. She kept yelling at him to "Just get in!" and he just kept crying and screaming "Noooo!" The mother reasoned, "Look! The teacher's right there in the pool. He'll catch you. Go ahead and jump! It'll be fine." But the youngster held his body stiff and screamed even louder.

What the mother failed to appreciate was that the little boy's response was cannily appropriate. He knew he couldn't swim and he had no proof that the teacher would catch him. He knew that when he threw things into water, sometimes they floated—and sometimes they sank to the bottom.

I wished the mother would have congratulated her son on his good instincts and affirmed that he was smart to sense that it isn't safe to jump into the water if you can't swim. Then she could have sat down beside him on the edge of the pool, stuck her toe in the water, invited him to join her, and had him watch while another child jumped in and got caught—all while waiting calmly with him to make sure he felt safe.

Just like that mother, we insist that our leaders jump into the scary waters of asking for money, urging them to ignore their own guts, which warn of embarrassment and rejection. We should congratulate them on their reluctance, not get exasperated with them. They sense that something's not quite right—and they're correct.

When we look at the root causes of their fear, we may find that there are systems in our organizations that need tending. It's easy to point fingers and say the board isn't doing its job, or the staff isn't supporting the board. Those may be true, but they're only symptoms that something deeper and systemic needs to be repaired or refreshed. If we attend to those systems—named as barriers in the pages that follow—we can dissipate the fear. And our board members can become proud stewards and powerful ambassadors on behalf of the organizations they lead.

If we want everyone to do their part joyfully, it's best if both board and staff address those barriers together. Here's how.

How to Use This Book

Your organization may have already dealt with some of the topics in this book. If so, congratulations! Feel free to skip the chapters you don't need.

To figure out what you *do* need, check out the first few paragraphs of each barrier chapter—where you'll find a brief description of the problem—and the last paragraph of each, where I summarize the solution. If you've got that concept under control, move on!

I've arranged the barriers in the order in which a board member generally enters and experiences an organization (and, thus, the order with which he or she might run up against each barrier), but read them in whatever order you like. They are all inextricably intertwined, however, so you'll find that some concepts might be reinforced or revisited in more than one chapter.

Knowing how full your life is, I wanted to keep the body of this book short so it wouldn't take you long to read it. That means I've had to leave some meat off the bones in the main text. The shaded boxes in the narrative may flesh out some of the ideas.

You'll also find some short videos and sample documents on my website (www.susanhowlett.com), which offer even more detail. Check them out whenever it's convenient and use them as you wish.

Because I've been working in nonprofits for over 35 years—as a board member, development director, executive director, and consultant—I feel as if I'm in the trenches with you, which is why I sometimes use the words "we" and "our." I also use the words "board member," "trustee," and "leader" interchangeably. And when I say "support," I use it generically to include time, sponsorship, in-kind gifts of goods or services, or money.

If you feel your organization needs to address more than one of the barriers described here, test the waters and begin with the easiest one. You'll find some suggestions about where to start in the last chapter. Just don't try to change too much at once, and remember to take care of yourself in the process. Good luck!

For more copies of this book, go to www.susanhowlett.com.
Discounts are available for multiple copies.

BARRIER 1

EXPECTATIONS ARE UNCLEAR

When I ask board members during solicitation trainings why they're not happy about asking for money, they say they weren't told that it was an expectation when they were recruited for the board. No one said they were expected to give, and no one said they were expected to ask, whether it be for volunteer time, gifts in-kind, or money. In fact, any discussion of expectations (about attendance, leadership, or being an advocate for the cause) was minimized just to get them to say yes.

It's no wonder many board members feel like victims of bait and switch when they discover that not only is fundraising an expectation, but they're constantly being asked to make their own contributions (to the annual campaign, the workplace campaign, the event, or the major gifts effort). Some say that fundraising is all they're being asked to do all the time.

OVERCOMING THE EXPECTATIONS BARRIER

Clarify Commitments at Recruitment

Obviously, organizations need to let people know *during recruitment*, that all board members are expected to make their own financial contributions, and all board members are expected to participate in fundraising. We need to show them very clear job descriptions, go over each item on the description, and make sure they understand the implications of each before inviting them to join the board.

I suggest having three documents at hand:

1. *One that describes the role of the board as a whole*

2. *One that describes the expectations of anyone who serves on the board*

3. *One that is customized for each particular board member*

CLEAR BUT HARMFUL EXPECTATIONS

Sometimes I see expectations that are clear, but misguided. Some organizations have prescribed gift amounts that each board member is required to contribute each year. I discourage this practice, as I've seen people who would have been great board members decline the nomination because they couldn't afford it, while others, who could have afforded ten times that, give only the required amount because that's the *number* they heard during recruitment.

Another expectation I discourage is the annual "give-or-get goal," where you have to raise a particular amount if you can't give it yourself. This puts all the emphasis on getting money, at any cost, from any warm body, rather than on identifying appropriate prospects and helping deepen their relationship to the mission. The latter engenders long-term support, including volunteerism, ambassadorship, or gifts in kind, which may not count toward the give-or-get goal, but are equally important to the nonprofit.

What usually happens is that the people who are good at fundraising exceed the goal, while those uncomfortable with it simply don't do it —and there's no consequence. This builds resentment among the doers and guilt among the others—neither of which creates a healthy environment for philanthropy. Meanwhile, everyone's more worried about how gifts get credited than they are about the donors' relationships with the mission.

For the first document, I use the standard "Roles and Responsibilities of the Board" from BoardSource (see end of chapter). One of the items on that list is "ensure adequate resources," which means that no one escapes responsibility for the fiscal health of the organization. Another item on the BoardSource list includes the phrase, "Enhance the organization's public standing, clearly articulating the mission, accomplishments and goals to the public and garnering support from the community." That's what the *board as a whole* is responsible for in terms of fundraising.

For the second document, I offer a list of expectations that apply to *every single board member*, regardless of his or her position in the organization or the community. It says that each member is expected to attend every board meeting and retreat, represent the leadership at each of our events, serve on a committee, make a personal financial contribution, and participate in fundraising in the way that most suits them.

For the third document, I suggest a *customized* contract that each board member creates with the appropriate committee (nominating, board development, governance committee) and signs, taking one copy and leaving one for the record of the organization. This one says something like, "Because I am Lisa Leader, and I bring unique gifts to this board, I agree to the following commitments this year to fulfill my duties in fund development." (See a generic example at the end of this chapter, and samples from two nonprofits on my website at www.susanhowlett.com.)

Hold Members to Their Commitments...

If the first way to overcome this barrier is to create clear expectations and share them proudly at recruitment time, the second one is to hold people to their commitments. I would charge the appropriate committee with watching participation all year long. If leaders fall behind with their giving or their activity, a committee member can contact them to see if something has changed (Did they lose their job? Do they hate the committee chair? Have they committed to more than they can follow through on?) and offer whatever support would make their job doable. We usually wait until there's a crisis to check in with people, or until there's already resentment built up about their lack of follow-through.

Then at the end of each year, have the board development committee do individual performance reviews with trustees to see how they felt about their original commitments and their performances in relationship to them.

COMMITMENTS THAT MAKE THEIR HEARTS SING

I often make a comparison between finding the right jobs for people and making a loaf of homemade bread. In order to make a loaf of bread, someone has to till some soil, and someone has to plant the seeds. Someone needs to harvest the grain and someone must grind it into flour. Someone needs to mix the dough, shape it into a loaf, then bake it, slice it and serve it. It's not necessary for the person who loves to knead dough to have to drive a tractor, or vice versa. We can assign board members to tasks that make their hearts sing.

This shouldn't be about fault-finding, but about discovery. And it shouldn't be about just fundraising, but how fundraising fits into the scheme of things for the board as a whole and as individuals. Think of the conversation as a two-way exploration of how the organization's systems foster the board's work and how each board member is responding. The reviews should be conducted in the spirit of board members discerning how they can add optimal value in ways that suit them, thus helping the organization thrive.

...But Also Help Them Meet Those Commitments

Getting to know each member's motivations can help with joyful commitment. The board development committee might meet one-on-one with board members to plan how they will make their contributions throughout the year to maximum advantage. Perhaps he works for a company where he feels significant pressure to participate in the annual United Way campaign. Why not allow him to look like a model donor at work by making his entire year's pledge to you there? If you have a "Fund a Need" section in your auction, a member may want to be the donor who launches the process with a showy large gift. She may prefer to leverage other support by being an early donor to your major gift campaign or by offering a challenge pledge. Does she usually make her gift at the end of the calendar year by transferring stock? Or does she want to contribute early in your fiscal year to create momentum for others? Have these discussions with each board member so it feels like you're meeting their needs as well as the organization's.

One last item about clarity of expectations: I see a lot of board members try to get out of making a personal contribution by claiming the sponsorships they garnered from their employers as their own. I think it's important for board members to make financial contributions from their *own* resources, in addition to asking their employers to participate. Making one's own gift is a different emotional experience from getting someone else to give. And in groups where a rich culture of philanthropy pervades the organization, every board member has a personal stake in the group's success.

When leaders understand best practices in the nonprofit sector, and when they are clear about what the organization expects of them, they can assume their roles with more gusto. When they get to shape a "contract" that reflects their personal strengths and preferences, they will likely do what they've agreed to do. And when they understand that board and staff will hold each other accountable through a respectful and routine process, they will feel supported enough to do their job.

ROLES & RESPONSIBILITIES OF THE BOARD AS A WHOLE

1. Determine the organization's mission and purpose, including goals, means, and primary constituents served.

2. Select the chief executive and ensure that that individual has the moral and professional support necessary to further the goals of the organization, then periodically assess his or her performance.

3. Provide proper financial oversight, including developing an annual budget and ensuring that proper financial controls are in place.

4. Ensure adequate resources.

5. Ensure the legal and ethical integrity and maintain accountability. The board is ultimately responsible for ensuring adherence to legal standards and ethical norms.

6. Ensure effective organizational planning, actively participating in the overall planning process and assisting in implementing and monitoring the plan's goals.

7. Recruit and orient new board members, and periodically assess the board's performance.

8. Enhance the organization's public standing, clearly articulating the mission, accomplishments, and goals to the public and garnering support from the community.

9. Determine, monitor, and strengthen the organization's programs and services, making sure they are consistent with the mission and monitoring their effectiveness.

Source: *Boards on Fire: Inspiring Leaders to Raise Money Joyfully* by Susan Howlett
Adapted from BoardSource, www.boardsource.org

Elements of a Generic Board Member Job Description

Embrace the mission of the organization

Learn – and carry out – the legal responsibilities of the board

Learn enough about the organization to portray it accurately

Attend all board meetings, retreats and special events

Come to board meetings prepared to participate fully

Play a leadership role in at least one committee or task force

Make an annual personal financial gift according to your means

Help with fundraising efforts in whatever way is most appropriate

Serve as an ambassador between the organization and the community

Communicate clearly and respectfully, and support the decisions of the full board

Keep the administrator informed about concerns in the community

Exercise loyalty and confidentiality in dealings with the board

Support the organization and officers in times of controversy or crisis

Fulfill commitments on time

What Board Members Can Expect from the Organization

Clear and reasonable expectations

Consistent, timely communication from staff

Access to any information needed about the organization

Training, encouragement and strategic advice to carry out tasks

Respect for the time, views, and talents you offer to the board

Source: *Boards on Fire: Inspiring Leaders to Raise Money Joyfully*
© 2010 Susan Howlett, All rights reserved

SAMPLE OF A CUSTOMIZED BOARD MEMBER CONTRACT

Board Member: _____

Mission of the organization: _____

My commitment to the mission of this organization inspires the following pledge:

1) Personal Gift:

☐ I will personally contribute $_____

☐ I will make that gift in the following way:

   ☐ with a check or cash: monthly / quarterly / yearly

   ☐ you can charge my credit card: monthly / quarterly / yearly

   ☐ through my workplace campaign, using payroll deduction

   ☐ by transferring appreciated stock or other appreciated assets

2) Raising Money:

☐ I will take responsibility for stewarding relationships with current donors.

☐ I will take responsibility for cultivating relationships with prospects.

☐ I will personally approach cultivated prospects or donors to ask for a gift.

☐ I will accompany more experienced solicitors on donor visits.

☐ I will call existing donors to ask them to renew their support.

☐ I will introduce the organization to #__ contacts from my circle of influence.

☐ I will approach those individuals through

   ☐ personalized letters

   ☐ telephone calls

   ☐ e-mail messages

   ☐ a house party or office party

   ☐ personal visits

☐ I have access to the mailing list of the following club, organization, spiritual group, employee group, fraternal association, professional association, trade union, or subscription list: _____

☐ I will write support letters to companies or foundations where I have contacts.

☐ I will accompany the Executive Director on a visit to a potential grantor.

☐ I have contacts with the following corporations or foundations:

Source: *Boards on Fire: Inspiring Leaders to Raise Money Joyfully*, 2010 Susan Howlett.
Adapted from a contract created by Octavia Morgan of the International Gay and Lesbian Human Rights Commission. Printed in the Grassroots Fundraising Journal, 1998.

3) In-Kind Contributions
- ☐ I will make the following in-kind contribution _____
- ☐ I will solicit in-kind contributions from others with whom I have contact.

4) Major Events
- ☐ I will help find a sponsor for: the fall event / the spring event
- ☐ I will be a table captain (securing 9 guests) to the spring event
- ☐ I will serve on the planning committee of: the fall event / the spring event
- ☐ I will secure #___ volunteers to support: the fall event / the spring event
- ☐ I will help with: set up / clean up / greeting / decorations / rides

5) Committees
I will serve on the following committees:
Finance / Board Development / Advocacy / Communications

6)Media Work
- ☐ I am willing to contact reporters, editors or producers to pitch stories
- ☐ I am willing to write letters to the editor in conjunction with staff
- ☐ I am willing to write content for our newsletter or website
- ☐ I have personal contacts with _____

7)Advocacy
- ☐ I am willing to reach out to elected officials to discuss our issues
- ☐ I am willing to attend / speak at public hearings or coalition gatherings

8) Other
- ☐ I am also willing to contribute in the following way(s)

Signature _____ Date _____

These commitments will be reviewed during the year with the Board Development Chair.

Source: *Boards on Fire: Inspiring Leaders to Raise Money Joyfully*, 2010 Susan Howlett.
Adapted from a contract created by Octavia Morgan of the International Gay and Lesbian Human Rights Commission. Printed in the Grassroots Fundraising Journal, 1998.

BARRIER ②
THE CONTEXT IS CLOUDY

Leaders consistently tell me, proudly, that their organization is the only one in the community addressing a particular issue or offering their particular service. The only trouble is that I have often consulted with three other organizations within 15 miles of them who do very similar work.

We do our board members a disservice when we don't paint a larger picture of the landscape for them. How can they lead or represent our organizations well if they don't know

- the problem or opportunity they're trying to address;

- the root cause of the situation and how it has evolved over time;

- which other organizations have been working on the topic, and what their experiences have taught us;

- how our work is distinct from other groups, and how our work enhances or augments theirs;

- the rationale for choosing our particular approach (Is there research proving the efficacy of this model, was it due to the availability of trained staff or volunteers, is it the cost per person served with this model vs. another, are we choosing to go upstream vs. putting on a band aid.);

- how the legislative or political climate, economic environment, and demographic shifts are affecting our work;

- whether our efforts have altered the situation over the past few years, and, if so, whether we are seeing small changes or sweeping ones; and/or

- what challenges keep us from being as successful as we'd like to be.

If they don't understand the context within which we work, leaders can't justify the need for our efforts and the place we hold in the constellation of organizations working in the same area.

Overcoming the Context Barrier

Explore the Landscape Together

We can help board members understand the landscape better by asking them to explain it to their peers. I understand that the staff already knows this information and has undoubtedly shared it with the board on numerous occasions, but that doesn't mean the board members heard it or internalized it.

Contextual information may indeed have been shared in a lengthy report by the executive director or a program staffer, buried in a written document, or offered in a way that didn't capture the board members' attention. Or maybe they didn't think it was essential to grasp it, so they sort of checked out during the presentation. They might not have understood how the information affected the health of the organization or their ability to lead it. So it didn't stick.

But if they have to learn the information well enough to report it back to their peers, they'll take it seriously and do a creditable job. They will also remember what they learned, and bring it up later in the year, when it's germane to a board discussion.

In preparation for a board retreat, I once had board members research the likelihood of continued funding from the city, the county, and the state. We chose members who had political connections in each of those administrations, so they could call people they already knew to get the answers. They discovered that the outlook was discouraging on all three levels, and that they would need to raise money from private sources the following year to meet their budget. The executive director had been telling them that for some time, but they didn't *hear* it until they were responsible for sharing their findings with their peers.

Consider assigning individual board members the task of learning some of this contextual information themselves, and then sharing their findings with the rest of the board. Ask them to talk with staff members in your organization, with leaders of similar organizations, or with the staff of public-policy makers. Have them search online or at the library for information about the field you're in. And when they present it, encourage them to use engaging formats such as pie charts, bar charts, photos, timelines on butcher paper, or audio or video from their interviews.

Create Opportunities for Discovery

Here are some other ways to engage board members in shared learning, to better help them understand the context of the organization's work:

- Take (or send) one or two of them on a road trip to visit other organizations who do similar work, and have them talk with board or staff there. (For example, an animal shelter I worked with took board members to all the other shelters in the region to see what distinguished each from the other and hear about trends in the field.)

- Pay for a member to attend a conference where she hears people talk about issues across the field or sector. (I knew a low-income housing developer who took a board member to a statewide conference where he heard a national speaker, met leaders from a dozen other organizations like his, and got great ideas to share with his board.)

- Offer to send (or take) them to a workshop or training on the topic. (A social service agency could take a board member to a United Way workshop on grassroots advocacy.)

- Ask them to help host a gathering of other organizations where the larger context is discussed. (I know of an environmental group that invited five other groups to an evening salon where leaders discussed the growing number of toxins in schools.)

- Invite someone to create a timeline showing how long the issue has been around and what milestones have occurred along the way. (One board member in a women's health organization codified all the victories and defeats in the fight for abortion rights over the last 100 years, putting the current struggle in perspective.)

- Assign them to read a relevant book with you and report on it to the rest of the board. (A group dealing with dyslexia once had board members read a novel with vivid descriptions of what it's like to be dyslexic, and offer their reactions.)

- Invite them to read and summarize articles from professional publications, research papers, topical blogs, or websites.

Some of my clients have invited outside experts or influential people to make presentations at their board meetings. The information presented may well help contextualize the organization's work, but there often isn't time for a generative board conversation to follow the presentation, so the board members are, once again, sitting back with their arms folded, listening and nodding, but not necessarily internalizing the information. Better to have one of them interview the expert and report on it themselves.

When planning board-member presentations, schedule each for a board meeting when that topic is featured on the agenda, so the new-found knowledge illuminates a timely discussion.

These assignments will

- deepen each member's overall understanding of the landscape;

- give them more things to discuss with prospects and donors; and

- make it easier for leaders to tie donors' varying interests to the mission, because they'll have more points of entry into the conversation.

Seeing the larger context will discourage board members from saying, "We're the first…, biggest…, only…" and explain instead, "This issue is so big, it takes the work of many nonprofits to address it. Here's the part *we're* playing in the interconnected web of our field."

The more they understand about the environment within which your organization works, the more they lean into leadership. And the more they lead, the more eager they are to raise money to address the larger issue in the community, not just the routine activities of your organization.

BARRIER ③

THE BOARD DOESN'T OWN THE BUDGET

Ask board members to call out the annual budget of the nonprofit they lead, even in broad terms ("Is it more like $100,000 or $1,000,000?"), and most of them will look at the treasurer. And when the group's financial statements get passed around, most don't know where their eyes should fall on the page, so they ask questions about recent expenditures, just to look like they're doing due diligence.

But it's not their fault. They haven't been told the most important things to watch for, and what strategic questions they should be asking about them. They don't know what factors determine the organization's fiscal health, or what the board can do to affect those factors. And they likely haven't had a hand in shaping the budget. It's no wonder they're uncomfortable asking for money, when they can't see or explain how someone's gift might affect the budget.

OVERCOMING THE BUDGET BARRIER

Make the Budget Decipherable

For starters, we should stop having CPAs come in to train our boards how to read financials. With all due respect to CPAs, they have a hard time translating budgets to finance-phobic folks. Instead, why not invite the treasurer from a highly functional nonprofit in your community to talk about how that board views its budget? Or have a banker or a foundation officer come in and explain to the board what they can tell about an organization by looking at its budgets or its income and expense statements. Board members need to be taught what patterns signal fiscal health and what things trigger red flags.

Once trustees have been shown what to look for, assign *them* to investigate and report on the organization's financial health, using pie charts and other visuals. They could look at the following types of things:

- What percentage of our income is earned, granted, and contributed?

- What percentage of the contributed income comes from individuals?

- What percentage of contributed income is generated by each fundraising method you use (events, mail, workplace, Web-based, major gifts, EFT, etc.)

- Where can board members have the most impact on revenue?

- How do our percentages compare with other healthy organizations—and what would be more sustainable targets for us to pursue?

Once, I sat on a board where a reluctant treasurer promised to lead the Finance Committee in a unique way during his term. He promised that the committee would be diligent about overseeing the organization's resources and it would report its progress at each board meeting. Each month, he would bring the financial statements, and if there was nothing amiss, he would put a smiley face at the top, and we wouldn't discuss them. If there was something that warranted attention, he would put a frowny face at the top, explain the aberration and tell us what Finance intended to do to rectify it—but we as a group still wouldn't discuss the statements themselves.

Instead of focusing on budget line items each month, we spent the allotted time discussing whether our budget truly reflected our mission, goals, and core values. The treasurer said, "A year from now, I want a stranger who picks up our budget off a sidewalk to be able to tell what we hold important." Those discussions were rich and satisfying, and they helped us reshape our budget so it told a story.

For one thing, our mission said that we promoted philanthropy, but you couldn't tell this from the financials, so we agreed to put money in the budget that we would give away, modeling philanthropy in our community. Our core values said we valued diversity in our organization, but you couldn't tell from the financials, so we created a program—with its own line item—to reach out to communities of color to attract and integrate more volunteers, members, donors, and leaders of color.

Finally, our goals called for more professional development for our members, but you couldn't tell this from the financials either, so we assigned some of the budget to scholarships to make continuing education accessible to everyone.

Can people tell what YOUR organization thinks is important by looking at your budget? If your leaders say they want to take good care of your human capital, the budget should reflect competitive salaries for staff and decent benefits, investments in facilitated retreats, professional development, celebrations, and awards.

Imagine your board having more conceptual—and less linear—conversations about how to allocate your precious resources. Help them investigate, report, and discuss the patterns in your finances. Allow your board members to be "trustees"—bestowed with the sacred trust to steward your resources responsibly.

As board members take ownership of the budget, now viewed in a larger frame, they begin to understand how they, as governors, can make the biggest impact. With the confidence gained from strategic conversations about a budget they've helped shape, they will proudly explain to donors how their gifts can affect the organization and the opportunities ahead of you.

BARRIER ④

TRUSTEES AREN'T ENGAGED IN GOVERNANCE

Most of the board meetings I attend as a consultant are disappointing. The main reason? The typical meeting structure offers little opportunity for board members to LEAD. Picture a conference room full of people with skills, talents, contacts, wisdom, experience, and passion for the mission— relegated to listening to a series of boring reports that aren't tied to a common vision or strategic goals. Fundraising is always the last item on the agenda, and it gets abbreviated or postponed because the other items took too long.

Instead of steering the meeting, leaders are leaning back in their chairs with their arms crossed, or furtively checking their messages.

There are many reasons why board meetings have ended up looking like this. One might be that strong executives don't really want their boards very engaged, because they've been burned by micromanagers in the past or they fear that a fired-up board might usurp some of their power.

Mostly, though, I think boring meetings are the result of benign neglect: whoever wants time on the agenda gets it and there's no overarching rationale for what the board spends its precious time on across the arc of a year.

One thing is for sure, though: no one wants to go out and raise money to fund committee reports.

Overcoming the Governance Barrier

The antidote to this problem is easy: create an environment where board members get to lead.

In their book, *Governance as Leadership: Reframing the Work of Nonprofit Boards*, the authors (Richard Chait, William Ryan, and Barbara Taylor) distinguish three modes in which boards operate: the *fiduciary* mode, the *strategic* mode, and the *generative* mode.

When they're operating in the fiduciary mode, boards are discussing things like budgets and contracts and legal responsibilities. When they're operating in the strategic mode, they're discussing things like goals and measurable outcomes, the relative merits of a collaboration, or what position to take on a legislative matter. When they're operating in the generative mode, they're temporarily suspending those other two modes, and thinking outside the box about how to address a systemic issue.

When I see boards operating in the fiduciary mode, their heads are down, their pencils are out, and they're looking at fine print, maybe even squinting. When I see boards operating in the strategic mode, they're sitting upright in their chairs, looking at one another. And when they get to the generative mode, they're leaning back in their chairs with their hands behind their heads, saying, "What would happen if we thought about it *this* way?" Their view is beyond the room's walls and the conversation is animated and engrossing.

If we created more opportunities for boards to have generative conversations, they would find the strategic conversations more contextual and satisfying, and they would lean into the fiduciary conversations eagerly because the financial and legal topics would feel vital to accomplishing the big ideas they created up front.

Fundraising then becomes a natural step in the process of achieving the vision they "birthed" in a generative conversation.

Design Meetings People Look Forward To

Here's how to shift the content of your board meetings so leadership can emerge naturally. Imagine a board meeting with an agenda that unfolds like this:

- An opportunity to build community among the board members

- An inspiring reminder of the organization's mission

- A vote on a "consent agenda"

- An opportunity for education or training of board members

- A generative conversation about a matter of consequence

Let's look at these steps in more detail.

1 First, building community increases accountability. When people don't know or care about the others in the group, they don't feel bad about dropping the ball on their assignments. But people who feel emotionally connected to one another follow through because they don't want to disappoint their peers. Here are some ways to build community:

- **Food**: I think every board meeting should have food, partly as a gesture of reciprocity because the leaders are volunteering their time, and partly to ensure that people's biological needs are met so they can pay attention. I also think something visceral happens when people break bread together. Some groups rotate the food assignment among board members; others assign food to staff. Check my website (www.susanhowlett.com) for a list of ways to handle food so it isn't a burden to anyone.

- **Introductions**: Begin your meetings with members restating their names (I've worked with boards where some people didn't even know their fellow members) and sharing a simple fact about themselves: their favorite movie, their favorite book, their favorite ethnic restaurant, a memorable trip, where they went to high school, or something more mission-related, such as their favorite children's book (literacy), their favorite historic building (preservation), their favorite park or trail, animal, boat, etc. This gives the others a little glimpse into each leader's personal life without taking time out of the meeting.

2 Second, it's important to remind people of the group's mission at every meeting to keep their leadership inspired. Sometimes, board members who are deeply engaged in committee work forget to tie that work to the larger mission and vision. In some organizations, I've seen staff share a story about someone who has benefited from their work, but I think it's more effective to have a board member responsible for the "mission moment." Rotate who shares one of these moments each month (and be sure to make it easy for them to connect with an end user). By learning a story well enough to share it with their peers, it will sink into their hearts and guts and they'll remember it for a long time. At the end of the year, board members will have heard enough stories that they'll feel really connected to your mission.

❸ Third, with a consent agenda, the staff puts into one document all of the reports and routine items that normally take up meeting time yet don't require board discussion (for example, the CEO's report, finance report, committee reports, or perfunctory ratifications). This document is sent out ahead of time with the expectation that everyone reads it before coming to the meeting. Then all items are voted on at once, becoming the official record of the organization.

A consent agenda eliminates from the discussion anything that already happened in the past and allows the board to spend the meeting time looking forward and applying their wisdom to important matters. You can find more information about consent agendas at www.susanhowlett.com/boards-on-fire/.

❹ Fourth, include 20 minutes of education or training so board members can anticipate learning something germane every time they attend a meeting. Knowing that the organization is investing in their ability to lead well will inspire them to use their newly acquired wisdom and skills. Here are a couple of points to remember:

- Think about *education* in terms of your line of work. Have a staff member or local expert come in to talk about trends or best practices in the field. Invite a board member who knows a lot about something (the legislature, collaboration, a sister organization they used to lead) to share his expertise. Education helps put your work in a larger context so the board can see how your organization fits into the broader community.

- Think about *training* in terms of how to be a more effective board member. If no one knows how to read the financial statements, train them on where their eyes should fall on the page and which strategic questions they should be asking. If they don't know how to work a room on your behalf or ask unapologetically for money or auction items, have someone show them how to do it. We need to stop complaining about what leaders do badly and give them the tools to do it better.

❺ Now imagine that those first four agenda items take 30 minutes total. That leaves you a good 60 minutes to engage in a deep, rich, satisfying conversation about something that matters, preferably something that relates to your strategic goals. Perhaps a task force went away after the strategic planning retreat to hammer out a recommendation on some topic. Give them a few minutes to outline their ideas and then open it up to the whole board to discuss. (See a list of topics other organizations have discussed during their generative conversation period on my website, www.susanhowlett.com. A great conversation starter is Jan Masaoka's insightful article "Governance and Support," which you can find at www.susanhowlett.com/boards-on-fire/.

Good board meetings help leaders feel as if the organization has invested in them, and they've invested in the organization. As meetings engage board members in rich, satisfying conversations about topics that further the mission, vision, and strategic goals, trustees can see how their efforts to raise money affect the organization. When board members are engaged in authentic leadership, they'll be eager to ask for financial support.

BARRIER 5

THE MISSION IS MUDDY

I often open a board retreat or training by asking the board members if they can tell me the mission statement of the organization they lead. Usually, they look around nervously, hemming and hawing until someone says, "Isn't it on the brochure? It must be in the bylaws. Who has a copy? " They start rifling through papers while someone else says, "I can tell you *generally* what it is."

After that person stumbles through a few sentences, someone else corrects her, and someone else chimes in with, "Bruce should know. He's the one who wrote it a few years ago for that grant." Sighing, the executive director reminds everyone that it's printed in their board notebooks—but no one has theirs with them. When someone finally does find the mission statement, it's usually boring or really long (or both), or it describes the activities the organization engages in, but not the *why*. Regardless, no one can repeat it.

If board members can't state the mission of the organization in an instant, they can't be using it to inform decisions they're making at board meetings. And if they can't describe the organization's ends at a Rotary meeting or a party or the lunchroom, how can they invite others to participate in or support our work?

Overcoming the Mission Barrier

Help Members Own the Mission Statement

Board members who have recently engaged in a conversation about the organization's purpose tend to bring it up whenever there's an important decision on the table, whether it's about launching a new initiative, serving a different constituency, or resolving a dilemma. And when board members have helped define with great clarity who you serve, and toward what end, they can repeat that compellingly to others.

While you will likely hear resistance to the following suggestion, I urge you to review your mission statement or engage the leadership in a conversation about your purpose at least once every year. People need to be reminded of the reasons you chose the words you did, and of the ramifications of those choices. (Are you doing this work *with* your stakeholders, as in organizing and mobilizing them to solve their own problems? Or are you doing the work *for* them, because you don't think they're in a position to solve their own problems? There's a big difference.) New board members who didn't participate in the generative conversation that produced the mission need to be caught up and motivated to lead using it.

If you want to hammer out a clear one-sentence mission statement that everyone on the board and staff is excited about in just 90 minutes, you can find instructions for a great interactive exercise on my website, www.susanhowlett.com. There's also a list of mission statements that were created using the exercise.

USE THE MISSION STATEMENT!

Once the mission statement has been adopted, keep it in front of board, staff, volunteers, and donors by putting it everywhere:

- on the top of agendas for board, staff, and committee meetings

- on the website, perhaps on each page

- on the signature lines of e-mails

- in the newsletter

- in the annual report

- on the wall in the conference room or entry way

- on people's business cards

- on thank-you notes

Have someone read it out loud at the beginning of meetings and retreats, and deputize a couple of board members to be the "mission police" at board meetings, asking when appropriate, "How does this further our mission?" or "What does our mission tell us to do here?"

Ultimately, you'll want to use the mission statement to shape your fundraising efforts and messages. Board members should be able to articulate the mission to every prospect they visit with, and be able to show that person how the funds you seek will help further the mission.

Conversations similar to the mission exercise should be held periodically concerning the organization's vision for the next few years, and the core values that will guide that journey.

When leaders have engaged in heady conversations about your aims, your audience, your vision, and your values, they'll use the results to lead, and they'll use them to share the essence of your work with donors and prospective donors. When board members feel ownership of the mission, they're proud to ask others to support it.

BARRIER ⑥
GOALS AREN'T DRIVING BEHAVIOR

When I'm helping board members get more comfortable with asking others for support, I often ask them what they want the money for. As you can imagine, they usually suggest that it's to run the organization, but they can't tell me what near-term goals the money could pay for.

Their inability to articulate the goals can stem from many factors:

- There *aren't any* goals.

- There are *so many* goals, no one can remember them.

- The board didn't really participate in the process of setting the goals (perhaps they were crafted by staff, a consultant, or a smaller group).

- The goals are part of a plan that isn't being used regularly to drive behavior (the proverbial "strategic plan on a shelf").

- The goals don't coincide with an organizational vision for the future.

- The intentions aren't really strategic goals for the entire organization, but more of an operating plan for staff.

- The targets have no bearing on the board's work, so it's easy for them to look at the goals and say to the director, "How are *you* doing with those?"

- The goals are so general that no one can measure whether you've reached them, such as "serve more people," "preserve more land/ buildings," "grow the audience," "raise more money," or something about "excellence.")

- The aims are so ambitious no one can imagine achieving them.

- They aren't bold or galvanizing enough to engender enthusiasm and motivate action.

If board members don't have a clear understanding of what they're raising money for, it's hard for them to convince others to support your work. They may not even trust, in their own hearts, that the money will be spent well or accomplish anything.

OVERCOMING THE GOALS BARRIER

Involve Trustees in Goal Setting

You can address this by engaging the trustees in a goal-setting exercise. To prepare for it, give each board member a homework assignment that will illuminate the current state of affairs and inform their discussion.

Make sure they get the support they need to succeed at the assignment. Send them Web links or articles so they don't have to start from scratch, and provide contact information for the people they're to interview. Be clear about what's expected of them. How long should their report be: three minutes or five? Do they need to bring copies for everyone? Describe what kind of visual will present their information most clearly: a pie chart, a bar chart, or a timeline?

At first, board members may be reluctant to accept the assignments because they suspect they're busy-work, and they don't understand what difference they'll make, but once they get into it, they get excited about what they're learning, and they're eager to share their findings with their peers.

Have people share the results of their assignments at a full board session. The reports will evoke animated discussions about important strategic matters, because board members might be grasping some concepts for the first time.

Having these assignments shared at a goal-setting meeting accomplishes many things:

- It ensures that board members will attend, because they have a role to play.

- It ensures that many voices will participate, not just the usual suspects.

- It ensures that they will make decisions based on data, not just opinions, impressions, or personal agendas.

- It means that the people who do the research will be the new resident experts on that topic, will remember what they learned, and will bring it up throughout the year when the topic comes up again.

- Best of all, it means they will care more deeply about the goals they set, which leads to more enthusiastic fundraising to meet the goals.

Here are some typical assignments. You'll find a longer list on my website, www.susanhowlett.com.

- Assign one board member to restate each of the previously set strategic goals and report how well the group has done achieving it.

- Assign several people to describe the various program areas in your organization, one member per program. Have each one answer a series of questions such as:

  - What percentage of the budget does the program represent?

  - How many people (or whatever) are served in a year?

  - Has that number gone up or down over the last three years, and is there more need than you're serving?

  - How many staff and volunteers does it take to run the program?

  - Where does its funding come from (e.g., grants, earned income, fees, contributed income) and what is it spent on (e.g., staff, supplies, equipment)?

  - What organizations or agencies do you cooperate with to make it happen and what is the relative health of those relationships?

- Assign a board member to find out which efforts you engage in each year to raise money (e.g., mail, phones, workplace, online, events, major gifts, etc.), the cost per dollar raised for each effort, the average gift for each, and the relative level of investment from board, staff, and volunteers.

Narrow the Focus

After the reports are shared, and people have had a chance to ask clarifying questions and get a handle on the implications of what they've learned, invite the leaders to identify their goals. I highly recommend limiting the number of goals so that everyone can remember them and use them to drive behavior. I usually suggest naming only three and in this order:

1. *One about the work you do (a program goal)*

2. *One about infrastructure (whatever you need in place to accomplish the program goal, whether that be physical plant, board, staff, committees, volunteers, policies, or systems)*

3. *One about finances*

If you don't insist that the board arrive at all of those three, you run the risk that they will set only programmatic goals, neglecting infrastructure and financial goals, which are just as important and take just as much time, effort, and resources. And, depending on the organization, the infrastructure and money goals really belong to the board, while the program goals belong, more or less, to staff.

(See my website for a simple goal-setting exercise, and examples of goals arrived at using the exercise.)

As you fine-tune the goals, encourage the leaders to make them SMART goals:

- Specific
- Measurable
- Achievable
- Realistic
- Timely (within a stated time frame)

Keep the Goals Alive

As you get more specific about how to achieve the goals, clarify which planning and implementation steps belong to the board and which belong to staff. Consider creating clearly defined deliverables for both board and staff so that no one is tempted to put all the burden of accomplishing the goals on the other party.

Once the goals have been determined, several things can be done to keep them alive and top of mind for both the board and staff.

1. *Use the goals to frame the agendas* of every board and staff meeting. If someone wants to put an item on the agenda that doesn't specifically further one of those goals, ask why you're devoting time to it. This keeps everyone focused on what you agreed were priorities.

2. *Reshape the committees* or work groups to reflect these goals, rather than trying to fit the work of the new goals into old committee structures that don't serve them.

3. *Base annual performance evaluations* for both board and staff on their progress with the goals.

If board members aren't reaching their development goals and don't seem too concerned about it, ask them to discuss which programs and staff people should be cut as a result. In one organization, we invited two affected staff to the board meeting, and asked the board to explain to them why they were about to lose their jobs. Yikes!

4. *Schedule big generative conversations* at board meetings over the next several months to discuss these topics.

Say that one of the goals was to move toward a more sustainable fundraising model. Have a task force or committee draft a plan and make recommendations for the full board to discuss. How delicious it will be to have a full hour at a board meeting devoted to that conversation, propelling you closer to your goal.

When board members create goals, based on their own research and their own wisdom, they will feel more ownership of them, and find it easier to ask others to support the work that will achieve those goals. And they'll express the need more urgently, more passionately, and more articulately.

BARRIER ⑦

OUTCOMES ARE VAGUE

When I ask board members what their organization does, they tell me about activities, programs, and projects. They seldom tell me what difference those things make. They can say *what* you do, but not *so what*.

Those who think to mention the impact do so in such global terms that listeners can't wrap their heads around it. They say things like, "We preserve our community's heritage," when what people really want to hear is the difference that makes for a child, an elder, or a newcomer to that community.

If board members are being asked to invite support, they need to be able to explain what impact the donor's gift could make on people, animals, the community, or the environment. If they can't, donors will gravitate to some other organization who can promise clearer results.

OVERCOMING THE OUTCOMES BARRIER

Help Trustees Paint Pictures

Here are two exercises you can do in just a few minutes at a board meeting to help members paint more vivid pictures about your outcomes.

- **So What?** Ask everyone to write down what difference they think your organization makes in the community or the world. Insist that they write it from the point of view of the end user or beneficiary of your work. What would those you serve say the organization is accomplishing? Have every trustee read aloud what they wrote, then discuss the relative merits of one another's statements, deciding which ones are most powerful.

  For example, I was once asked in a workshop to introduce myself to a stranger the way I usually did. I said that I worked for a center that engaged in prevention education, advocacy, early intervention, and clinical therapy for people who had survived sexual assault. After hearing that we should reframe our introductions to reflect the difference we made to end users —the "so what," not the "what"—I changed my introduction to "I make life safe again for four-year-olds who've been raped."

- **So That...** But sometimes, board members struggle with putting into words and imagery the difference we make. Ask them instead, then, to start by describing what you do, what activities you engage in or what programs you offer, and then write *why*—over and over again. It's called a "so that chain." Here's an example:

We teach illiterate parents to read, so that
They can read to their children at home at night, so that
The children are excited to learn to read at school the next day, so that
They might reach third-grade reading level by third grade, so that
They are more likely to graduate from high school on time, so that
They can become contributing adult members of our community.

Try this with every activity your organization engages in to see where the chains end up. The chain for every program or project ought to end in a similar place—and that place ought to reflect your mission. If board members all do this exercise together, and see and hear what their peers have written, collectively they will articulate more potent outcomes: ones they feel comfortable sharing with donors and prospects.

Imagine the thrill of seeing board members then align their "so that" chains or their "so what" statements with the mission statement they've crafted and the strategic goals they've set!

Help Trustees Tell Stories

Trustees will also be able to articulate the ultimate outcomes of our work if they are equipped with *stories* to share about what people's money looks like when it hits the street—when the mission comes to life in the community or the world. An old fundraising adage says, "Statistics raise eyebrows. Stories raise money."

In Penelope Burk's book, *Donor-Centered Fundraising*, we learn that donors would give us more money if we shared more stories that prove that their gift actually landed somewhere, touched someone, and made a difference. We must regularly equip our board members with these stories of impact, and help them learn how to share them in the most powerful way.

Trustees who have gone through interactive exercises to clarify what difference the organization makes—and by extension what difference a donor can make—feel empowered and proud to share those results with others.

BARRIER 8

THE FUNDRAISING STRATEGY IS ILL-DEFINED

I hear regularly from staff, impatient with board members who won't raise money when it's obvious there's a budget shortfall, or frustrated with leaders who want to sell some product or put on an event without considering how much staff time and effort would be involved.

It's inappropriate, though, to get upset with leaders who don't jump in when we think they should, if it's not clear how their participation fits into the overall development strategy. Likewise, getting upset with board members who mean well but go off in the wrong direction does no good. The problem is not the board, but the lack of a coherent development strategy.

Board members can feel it in their hearts and in their guts when the strategy doesn't make sense. Their natural reaction is to shut down, refuse to participate, or resort to unsuitable tactics they've seen in other settings.

Overcoming the Strategy Barrier

Help Board Members Learn Best Practices

Even the most sophisticated organizations sometimes lose sight of the fundamental concepts that shape good fundraising. We can all benefit from periodically refreshing our understanding of the field's best practices, which are grounded in research.

Here are six concepts that I've found most effective in helping organizations focus their fundraising strategy:

1. Spend more time generating contributed income than granted income.

2. Pay the most attention to the people closest to the organization, not new donors and not rich people.

3. Prioritize retaining and upgrading current donors, and retrieving lapsed donors over acquiring new donors.

4. Focus your attention on donors who have given the most money.

5. Invest more energy deepening donors' relationships with our work than asking, and ask only when we know people are ready to say yes.

6. Emphasize lower-cost-per-dollar-raised methods rather than high-cost efforts.

Let's expand on each of these concepts.

1. Contributed income is more sustainable than grants.

Board members like to think that grants are the answer, because someone else writes something down and sends it away somewhere—to people whose job it is to give away money. Grants distance us from the process and they feel like "easy money." Here are some things we need to remember about grants:

- Only about 10 percent of all charitable giving comes from grants.

- Grants are not a repeatable, sustainable revenue stream because funders change their guidelines regularly or stipulate that you can't apply again once you've been funded.

- Most grantors won't fund operating expenses, which is what you need most.

- You can write the best proposal in the world and still not get funded because there are many other factors over which you have no control.

- Grants take enormous amounts of time and effort, identifying appropriate sources, building relationships with them, preparing to apply, writing the proposal, complying with their requirements, tracking and reporting outcomes and expenditures, and offering recognition and stewardship.

- Grantors expect nonprofits to raise most of their budgets from contributed income and they ask how you plan to generate support from individuals to carry on whatever they fund.

One way to help leaders understand these points is to invite a current or former grantor to a meeting to explain the role of grants in the nonprofit sector, and why it's irresponsible to expect grants to fund the majority of your work.

2. Pay the most attention to the people closest to the organization.

It's much easier to raise money from people who already know who you are, understand what you do, and think it adds value in the community than it is to approach strangers. We should be focusing our attention on people who have already "leaned in," indicating that they're interested in your cause. Before reaching out to anyone new or simply wealthy, look to your core constituents:

- Your board
- Your staff
- Your volunteers
- Your current donors (anyone who's made a gift in the last year)
- Anyone who benefits directly from your work and knows it

These are the people who understand deeply why you do what you do, and who have the most investment in your success. If they're not giving generously and modeling that behavior to others, why would anyone else consider supporting you? We insult people when we decide for them that they won't want to give because they're already giving their time or they don't have much money. Offer these stakeholders the same information you'd give to anyone else, and let them make up their own minds.

Our next prospect pool is anyone who has been touched by our work, but is not in the core group mentioned above. This includes anyone who was ever board, staff, volunteer, client, student, audience member, or donor. They have all said yes to you at some point, so they're more prepared to give than a newbie.

Also consider people who attended something you were involved in (tour, concert, educational program, or hearing) but who aren't as close to you as those who've been more engaged (such as friends of board members). Include here vendors, professional allies, and extended families of those who have been served by your organization. (Please see the related circle diagram on page 54. For more information, see the explanatory video on my website, www.susanhowlett.com.)

3. Prioritize retaining and upgrading current donors, and retrieving lapsed donors, before reaching out to new ones.

Recent research by Penelope Burk revealed that retention rates among donors to nonprofits are staggeringly low. Many nonprofits are losing half of

Board
Staff
Volunteers
Current donors
Those directly served

Former board   Former staff

Service clubs

Former volunteers

Lapsed donors

Those served in the past

Those indirectly served

Businesses

Non-donor attendees at gatherings or events

Leaders and donors of organizations with similar missions or constituencies

Professional associates

Friends of the core constiuents

Foundations

Family of core constituents

Employers of core constituents

Vendors

Government funders

People who might be interested but have no awareness or contact yet

their donors each year due to simple neglect! Yet it costs much less to keep our current donors than to attract new ones—so why are we spending so much time and energy on acquisition instead of trying to keep the people who have already said yes?

Our No. 1 goal needs to be retaining current donors. Our second goal should be investing in our relationships with current donors so they'll want to give us more. And third, we should be retrieving lapsed donors who gave recently, but not this year.

4. Focus attention on your top donors.

Since the top 20 percent of the donors in most organizations are giving 80 percent of the money, it's a good idea to keep those donors happy. Their support alone is practically enough to sustain the organization. Focusing attention on major donors makes sense for several reasons:

- Losing one major donor is more of a blow to the budget than losing many small donors.

- Retaining major donors costs less than wooing them back after they've left.

Donor Pyramid

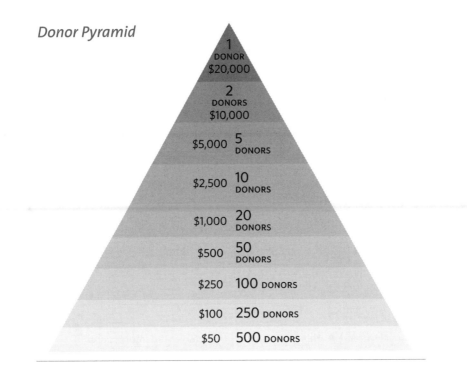

- Keeping current major donors costs less than acquiring new ones.

- If they're happy and well cared for, they'll be more inclined to introduce others to the organization.

(Please see the pyramid diagram above. For more information, see the explanatory video on my website.)

5. Work on deepening people's relationship with the cause rather than simply asking them for money—and ask only when they're ready to say yes.

People go through a series of stages as they become donors, then repeat donors, and then major donors to organizations. It's the same cycle consumers go through when they buy a product and then become loyal buyers. We understand that process intuitively and know that if we win someone's loyalty authentically, they'll renew their support of their own volition.

Development professional Buck Smith captured this process in a construct he called Moves Management. If we take each of the five steps in Moves Management in order, the relationship unfolds organically and everyone enjoys it. The process includes the following steps:

- Identification—During this phase we identify our most likely prospects (those closest to the organization) and learn enough about them to have a pleasant conversation.

- Information—Here we clarify for the prospects what issue or opportunity needs attention, what can be done about it, what will be different if we address it, and what's in it for them or the community.

- Interest—In this stage, we pay close attention to see if the prospect is participating in the conversation. Is he calling the office with questions, responding to our online survey, sticking around after a program or event, indicating that he's curious about our work?

- Involvement—At this point, those who are interested usually get physically or emotionally involved, making an in-kind gift of goods or services, volunteering in some small way, attending something, or participating in a task force or focus group.

- Investment—At this stage, once they've indicated interest and they've gotten involved, it's time to offer the prospect an opportunity to contribute.

Once the donor has given, it's important to take her back through the cycle, showing her the difference her gift made, introducing her to another facet of the work, and watching for increased interest. Then we can offer more sophisticated opportunities for involvement and more strategic opportunities to contribute.

Organizations who spend more energy and resources on relationship building than asking make more money, and their donors stay longer and share their excitement with others. We should avoid the mistake of going straight from identifying a good prospect to asking for money before it's time. (Please see the Moves Management diagram here. For more information, see the explanatory video on my website.)

6. Engage in efforts with lower costs per dollar raised.

If you documented all of your out of out-of-pocket expenses, all the staff time, and all the board and volunteer time that went into each of your fundraising efforts (appeal letters, workplace campaigns, Web-based giving, events, major gifts, etc.), you would see a clear pattern: the cost per dollar raised is highest for events, and lowest for personal solicitations. Big events are the most expensive way there is to raise a dollar!

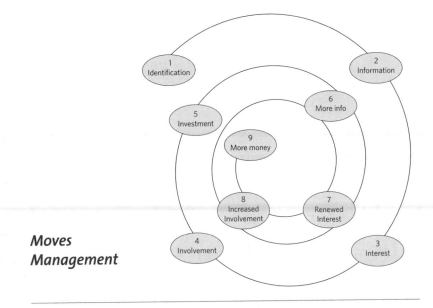

Moves Management

Diagram labels:
1 Identification
2 Information
5 Investment
6 More info
9 More money
8 Increased Involvement
7 Renewed Interest
4 Involvement
3 Interest

People push back whenever you share this information, insisting that there are so many other reasons to have the event. But if the same number of people hours were spent cultivating relationships with current donors, you could raise much more money with the same amount of effort. Once they realize this, responsible board members usually see that moving toward lower cost-per-dollar-raised efforts—like simply asking people for money—is the best strategy in the long run for the board, for the staff, for the donors, and for the organization.

> If people insist on holding an event, have them articulate and priori-tize their non-fundraising goals, then quantify and measure them after the event to see if it was worth it. If you can't quantify and measure the benefits of the event, you should question why you're investing so much energy in it. (See my website for a list of other reasons to have an event, and how to measure the results.)

When board members understand best practices in the field and see a development strategy that aligns with the fundamental principles of fund-raising, they'll be more willing to participate. Part of their resistance may have been justified if they were being asked to follow a strategy that didn't make sense.

BARRIER ⑨

THE BOARD ISN'T BEING USED OPTIMALLY

Sometimes when I'm leading a board training, I'll ask, "So, what are board members being asked to DO to raise money?" People usually look around at one another and no one says anything until finally, someone replies, "Well, we're supposed to fill tables at the gala—is that what you mean?" And someone else says, "We're supposed to get sponsors, too." But no one can ever just nail it and say, "These are the five things we're asked to do each year."

Most board members don't know precisely what it is that they can do to add optimal value in fund development. And even when they DO know, the things they're being asked to do aren't necessarily the best use of their position. Decision makers in any organization are powerful assets and should be used carefully and strategically.

> I was once in a meeting with a board president who was the CEO of a large, prominent corporation. She said, "Don't ask me to do penny-ante fundraising. Save me for surgical strikes." When the executive director asked for clarification, she said, "If you need someone to call the governor and get a return call that day, I can help you. Please don't tell me I have to sell raffle tickets."

Board members are a precious commodity in our organizations, and we need to assign them to tasks that befit their role. We often look at them as glorified volunteers and set them to work marking off the road for the fun run when the most important thing they can be doing is connecting prospects and donors to the mission. If we gave them jobs that warranted their attention, they might rise to the occasion.

Use Your Donor Pyramid

The donor pyramid (see page 55) can be a useful tool for visualizing where board members can have the biggest impact on fundraising.

Near the *bottom of the pyramid*, we might have people who have just made their first gift. Imagine how impressed they'd be if they got a call from a board member, a day or two later, welcoming them to the organization, asking how they heard about it, asking how they'd like to plug in, and offering to make a connection for them or invite them on a tour. Donor retention might increase if new donors got that sort of treatment!

Also near the *bottom of the pyramid*, board members could invite people from their circles of influence to attend a reception, open house, annual meeting, or educational program that would introduce them to the organization without any mention of a request. They could watch to see who acts interested, and follow up with them as appropriate, watching for clues before asking for a financial gift.

Near the *middle of the pyramid*, there may be donors who don't make major gifts but who have given consistently for a long time. Keeping those donors connected, affirmed and engaged is a great use of board energy, and safe too! Often, those small but consistent donors are the ones who include your group in their wills.

And at the *top of the pyramid*, periodic value-added contact between board members and high-level donors can generate more revenue with less effort than anything else in the strategy. You'll find specific suggestions in the story on page 75.

Penelope Burk's research revealed that donors really want only three things, which, by the way, they are not getting:

- Prompt, personal, meaningful thank-you cards (not form letters on letterhead that arrive late and talk about the organization)

- Assurance that their gift is being spent as promised or requested

- Proof that their gift made an impact after you spent it

Board members want to add value. They want to help sustain the organization. Let's focus their attention on the donors and prospects with whom even a little effort by a trustee can make a big difference. Let's put them to the best use possible—building relationships by welcoming and thanking people, showing them how their gifts were used, involving them in our work—using the lowest cost, most personal means.

When board members are enlisted to invite stakeholders into deeper connection with our work, they will participate more joyfully in fundraising. You'll find more on this topic on my website, www.susanhowlett.com.

BARRIER ⑩

LEADERS AREN'T EQUIPPED TO BE AMBASSADORS

I often hear board members say, "I'd be happy to represent the organization in the community if only I had a decent brochure to hand people." They want a piece of paper or a fancier website to make the case for them, which diverts everyone's attention from donor contact by focusing resources on document design.

If leaders *are* willing to talk with people, they rely on a one-size-fits-all "elevator pitch," which they've proudly gotten down to three minutes! The only problem with that is that no one wants to listen to any pitch for more than ten seconds! And frankly, listeners would rather be talking themselves.

Unfortunately, our board members don't know who to talk to or how to engage donors or prospects in conversations about the other person's relationship to our mission. And they don't know how to tailor the conversation to a particular person, whether it's a legislator, a foundation officer, a corporate sponsor or a friend from work.

What people really want is a passionate champion who can articulate a compelling case for support. We're setting our leaders up to fail if we don't help them prioritize *who* to talk to, *what* to talk about, and *how*.

Overcoming the Ambassador Barrier

Clarify Who to Talk To

We tend to send board members off to tell everyone with a pulse about the organization. What they need from us is clarity about which donors and prospects should be the top priority for their attention.

I think we should first focus board members on being ambassadors to our current top donors or recently lapsed top donors; then people who have made gifts over several years, regardless of size; then people who have made small gifts but who have indicated great interest; then people who have connected with our work but are not yet donors. Only after that should they be asked to focus on strangers!

And if we're asking them to introduce strangers to our mission, we should be clear about what types of people are most likely to give. If there's a demographic profile or psychographic profile among your current donors, share that with your leaders so they can go find more people like that.

> If you're a coalition or alliance that does more systemic work (say, advocacy or legislative reform or precedent-setting legal cases), suggest that board members concentrate on more highly educated prospects who are more evolved as philanthropists and understand the value of systemic change over direct service.

Regardless of your mission, focus board members on prospect pools of people who are already used to giving, such as members of service clubs, members of faith communities, or people who give enthusiastically to their Alma Mater every year.

If you're asking board members to represent the leadership at one of your gatherings, tell them precisely who will be there, which donors or prospects deserve board attention, and how you'd like those people approached at that event. You might also initiate a new guideline that board members aren't to talk to one another at donor gatherings. Their job is to work the room, connecting with donors and prospects, not to be a guest at the party.

> One of my clients assigned board members to particular guests who were coming to their auction. Their job was to listen for the guests' bidder numbers, and if they purchased something significant, to go to their table and congratulate them, assuring them that their support would be put to good use right away. What a great way to employ board members as ambassadors!

Most important of all, if you're asking board members to introduce people in their circles of influence to your organization, teach them how to watch for lean-in as the prospects learn more about you, and not to push people to give who aren't exhibiting interest.

I once heard a wise board member talking about the concept of social capital. She had spent a lifetime building relationships throughout the community, earning a stellar reputation and the respect of countless people, many of them influential. She said that when nonprofits asked her to approach her contacts for money, they were asking her to spend her social capital on their behalf. She said she had to think long and hard about whether an organization was really worth her investment, as she was putting her reputation on the line. Are you spending your board members' social capital optimally?

Practice Asking Questions

We explored how to articulate your outcomes in Barrier 7. It's important to help board members talk more about outcomes than activities, more about stories than statistics, and more about who's served than the organization itself.

But even better than telling prospects things is training board members to ask open-ended questions. The best way to be a powerful ambassador is

One time I went to meet with a land trust on a beautiful island. They asked if they could share the pitch they made to potential major donors, and get my feedback on it, so I said "Sure!" They spent ten minutes talking to me about easements and other legal procedures they used to protect precious land for perpetuity. At the end they asked, "So how was that?" To which I responded, "Boring as can be!"

What they might have done was ask me if I ever vacationed there, and when I responded positively, they could have asked me what I liked about coming there. I would have told them that I live next to a freeway, so I love how quiet it is there. And since our family loves birdwatching, we love the old-growth forests, the wetlands, and the pristine beaches. All they had to say back was, "That's what we're trying to save." And the whole conversation would have been complete. No easements, no perpetuity. Just what *I* was interested in talking about.

to ask others about their relationship to the mission, and then connect your work with the prospect's answers.

Board members can be shown how to ask open-ended questions that elicit clues about how the prospect or donor might connect to the mission. My favorite starters include:

- Tell me about...

- What do you think about...?

- How do you feel about...?

Someone commented that those are "therapists' questions." It's true. The reason therapists use them is that they get the *other* person talking about himself. Then we can listen for how he connects to the mission, rather than us blathering on about things he doesn't care about.

For example, "Tell me how you got introduced to the organization in the first place" or "What do you think about the proposed new legislation?" or "How do you feel about that perpetually empty store front on Main Street?"

Spend some time at a board meeting crafting a bunch of open-ended questions that might work for your leaders, then type them up and make sure everyone has copies in preparation for their work as ambassadors.

Teach Them What to Talk About

Leaders also need to know how to articulate what's in it for the prospect to be part of our organization. What tangible and intangible benefits can we promise a donor who supports our work? Do they get access to information, people, or gatherings that non-donors don't get? How do our results further the donor's personal goals?

Research tells us that there are three things that motivate giving, and board members should understand how to weave them all into their conversations with donors and prospects:

- People want to feel appreciated, not just for gifts they've given in the past, but for their values, priorities, and actions in the world.

- People want to know that their behavior makes a difference. They need us to draw vivid pictures of what happens when people contribute to our work. Where did that gift land; whose life was touched?

- People are yearning for a sense of community or a sense of belonging. Board members can use words like *belong* and *community* and *family* to let them know how being part of our organization will help them belong to a group of people with shared values and shared interests.

Customize the Message

Boards can also be shown how to tailor messages to different audiences. We know from research published in *The Seven Faces of Philanthropy* that there are different donor types. Board members need to understand what those seven donor types are, how to spot them, and how to shape a message to meet that type's needs.

For example, one of the types is called an Investor. Investor donors want to hear us use the words "return" or "ROI." They want to know there's an audit and a strategic plan. They want to know what our deliverables are, and how we're measuring our success. They want to know that a timely investment in these at-risk youth will cost us all less than if they're incarcerated or on welfare ten years from now. If we don't use words they relate to when we discuss our organization, we might lose them as donors. Spend some time at a board meeting discussing the seven donor types and how to customize your message to each kind.

(See my website, www.susanhowlett.com, for more details on the seven donor types.)

Remember the "so that chain" we talked about in Barrier 7? It might be good to revisit your chain and see who cares about each layer, so board members can align their conversations with something that matters to each prospect.

Here's what I mean. Using the example in the earlier section, you could ask yourself, *who cares* whether the illiterate parents learn to read? Well, the parents do. Who cares whether they read to their kids at night? The kids do. Who cares whether the kids are excited to learn to read the next day in school? Their teachers. Who cares whether they're at third-grade reading level by third grade? The principal. Who cares whether they graduate on time? The school board and school district. And who cares whether they become contributing members of society? Employers, taxpayers, law enforcement, etc.

Sometimes, this exercise opens up new prospect pools, as when one person pointed out that the parents of other students in the classroom care whether the children in the chain are interested in learning.

If we're asking board members to represent us in the community, it's our job to prepare them for that job. They're not going to be good at it on their own.

When my son was in elementary school, the fourth graders reenacted a journey on the Oregon Trail. The kids had made period costumes and moccasins to wear, prepared hard tack and jerky to eat along the way, and packed only what settlers would have had with them before they walked ten miles across town, pulling their red wagons with makeshift schooner tops on them.

The school, understanding that this was an opportunity for a news story, called all the kids together the day before and said, "Tomorrow, people might come up to you with TV cameras, radio microphones, or newspaper reporters' notebooks, asking you what we're doing. Let's talk about what you might say so you'll feel prepared." Not surprisingly, the kids handled the assignment with grace and clarity. Are we setting up our board members with the same deliberate care?

As you equip your leaders with the tools they need to be great ambassadors, make sure they're not using negative, violent words when they talk about approaching prospects. Most of the words people use to describe fundraising create a hostile environment. Discourage leaders from using phrases like "hit them up," "twist their arm," "put the squeeze on them," and "lean on your friends," even in lighthearted banter. Instead, encourage words like "approach," "invite," "visit with," or "reach out to." (See my website for a long list of negative, violent words people use to describe asking.)

When board members have been shown how to prioritize with whom they should be visiting, what to talk about with them, and how to hold engaging, donor-centered conversations, they will become powerful ambassadors on our behalf. Knowing how best to connect another's passion to the mission gives them the confidence to represent our organizations compellingly. And they will.

BARRIER 11
TRUSTEES HAVEN'T SEEN GOOD MODELS

I'm called upon often to train board members how to ask for major gifts and before they turn the session over to me, someone usually says, "Now don't forget—we can't roll this campaign out unless we have 100 percent giving among board members, so if you haven't made your gift yet, be sure to write your check tonight and give it to the treasurer before you leave. Now, the next item on the agenda…"

That would not elicit a joyful major gift from me! How can we expect our trustees to make compelling requests when they haven't experienced a stirring invitation themselves? We must model great asking—with them!

Not only have they not been asked artfully, they may not have been thanked well, acknowledged appropriately, engaged more deeply, or inspired to contribute in a more sophisticated and intentional way.

Finally, we ask them to reach out to others without giving them the specific support they need to feel successful. We may give them procurement forms for the auction, or contracts to share with potential sponsors, but they still feel ill-equipped to approach people for support. Even though they're accomplished adults, they long for help deciding what to say to someone, or how to behave in a face-to-face request, or how to craft a memorable note. We assume that leaders are more prepared to cultivate and solicit than they really are.

Overcoming the Model Barrier

Treat Trustees As You Treat Major Donors

First, make sure each board member is being thanked, recognized, and stewarded well, so they feel their contributions are being honored and affirmed. They deserve hand-written thank-you notes, personal phone calls and verbal acknowledgement at all events.

If we want our trustees to be major donors, it pays to honor their myriad gifts to the organization on an ongoing basis. Forego the plaques and certificates. Instead, capture and reflect the unique contributions they've made throughout the year, as they would like them represented, even if their biggest contribution was to challenge everything. If they feel known and heard by an organization, they are more likely to treat donors and prospects the same way.

Engage the Board Before You Ask Them to Engage Others

Second, make sure they're being involved strategically, so they understand what it will feel like if they engage a donor the same way.

Sometimes, board members aren't giving generously or joyfully because they haven't been involved viscerally in the work or seen its impact. Perhaps they joined the board because a friend asked them, or they sought the cachet associated with the position, but they don't *really* understand what you do. We take for granted that they will support the organization, without ensuring that they are excited about the mission and our outcomes.

To engage your board members before asking them for financial contributions, consider these small steps:

- Invite each board member to write their own testimonial about why they care about your organization. They might struggle to articulate it, but it will be an insightful assignment.

- Have them gather stories to be shared at board meetings, in newsletters, in the annual report, on the website, and in appeal letters or thank-yous. As they collect and share stories from people who have benefitted from your work, they will gain a deeper understanding that the group really does make a difference.

- Make sure they've been on a behind-the-scenes tour, been given insider information, been told what difference their contributions have made, and gotten first-hand accounts of the mission at work.

- Offer them opportunities to offer advice or share their expertise, or open a door to an in-kind gift of goods or services.

Third, make sure they're asked powerfully for their own financial contribution.

Imagine each board member being taken out for coffee by another board member who thanks them for all the gifts they've made to the organization over the last year, including policies they've worked on, auction items they've procured, and mentorship they've offered to newer leaders.

Then they could say, "Now I'm asking you to make a financial contribution to this organization that is large enough that you have to go home and discuss it with your family. Large enough that you feel like it represents your deep belief in our work, that it signals to your children or your close friends that this is a priority in your life, and that it manifests to others that you're proud to lead this organization."

No one has to know the dollar amount. This conversation is about commitment, not money. And when they see what that feels like, they won't mind initiating the same conversation with others.

Finally, if you're asking board members to call someone on your organization's behalf, give them a script. If you're asking them to write notes to someone, suggest language. If you want them to share stories of impact, give them a crib sheet. Are they working some room on your behalf? Give them a list of questions to ask and help them practice using them. Don't assume that just because they're successful adults that they have all the tools to do what you ask of them.

When board members have been engaged in the mission, cultivated and stewarded well, and asked powerfully for their own personal gift, they will understand what it feels like to be a donor in that situation. Just as with children, they repeat the behavior they've experienced. Make sure what happens to them is intentional, strategic, personal, and respectful. Model the behavior you want them to exhibit and they'll emulate it with others.

Now we've looked at the main barriers that I think keep board members from raising money joyfully. Let's look at what happens when the barriers are removed.

Fundraising Joyfully:
How One Board Caught Fire

This is a true story of an organization that used the lessons here to help board members overcome their fears and experience the deep joy and satisfaction of fundraising done well.

A few years ago, I was called in to teach the board members of the Washington Trails Association (WTA) how to ask for major gifts. Several minutes into the training, I noticed that all the board members were looking pretty defensive, with their arms crossed and their faces expressionless. I stopped and said, "I'm getting some hostile vibes here, you guys. What's that about?"

One brave board member replied, "Well, no one ever told us we were going to have to do this when we were recruited for the board. We're not good at this kind of thing, it feels really uncomfortable, and we're not really willing to do it."

I thought about this for a moment and then said, "Well then, what if we said you didn't have to ask; all you had to do was take a couple of donors from the top of your donor pyramid (your inner circle) and take them around that Moves Management cycle?"

"That sounds like it takes a lot of time," one noted, "and we're really busy people, so that's probably not going to work either."

I responded with, "Well then, what if we asked you to call two top donors and simply thank them, on behalf of the board, for their past support?"

"Nah," they said. "Too scary."

"Why is that scary?" I queried.

"Well, we don't know those people, and just calling them feels sort of intrusive, and besides, they might ask us a question we don't know the answer to."

Not wanting to give up, I offered one more option. "What if we asked you to call two donors, when you KNEW they weren't going to BE there, and leave a voice mail?"

"YES," they cheered! "We can DO that!"

So we assigned each board member to two donors (any more than two and people's willingness evaporates), gave them a little background on their donors (e.g., whether they'd ever been on the board, attended events, or worked on a trail project—nothing about gift amounts), and offered them a script to use if they wanted.

The board members each dutifully called their two donors to leave a message, and what do you think happened? Most of the people answered their phones! Yikes!

The nervous trustees stumbled through their introductions, only to discover that the donors were really flattered to be getting a call from a board member. And when the donors realized that there was no request involved, they started talking animatedly about how much they loved Washington Trails, and how much they enjoyed supporting WTA's work.

The board members were incredulous! They came back to the next board meeting, saying, "Well that wasn't THAT bad. We could probably do one more thing with those people."

So we had the executive director craft a brief e-mail message—only a few lines long—that said, "If you're planning to go hiking this weekend, here are three trails where we've heard the wildflowers are amazing right now." All the board members had to do when they got it from the E.D. was hit "forward" on their computers to send it to the same two donors.

Realizing that this had taken only a few seconds to accomplish, the leaders came to the next board meeting willing to make another contact with their two donors. We quickly crafted a one-page flyer that said, "When you gave us money last year, you had no idea what difference it would make, but here are some stories to show you what your gift looked like when we put it to work." All the board members had to do was hand-write a note in the margin (staff suggested wording), hand-address it (staff gave them addresses), put on a first-class stamp (offered by staff), and mail it to their donors.

The next month, we held a private reception at a store that sells outdoor gear. Board members phoned their two donors to invite them to come, share some refreshments, meet a famous wilderness photographer, and see the photos from his forthcoming book. As it turned out, even the introverts had a good time!

A few weeks later, the board members invited their two donors to join the E.D., the program director, the trustees, and other major donors on a hike on a special trail. WTA had been working to keep that particular trail free from motorized vehicles and they wanted to show the donors why it was so precious. Everyone who came had a great time, and those who couldn't come asked to be included if such a hike happened again.

Soon after the hike, the E.D. read an article in a national trade publication which she thought the donors would find interesting. She sent two copies to each board member, instructing them to highlight what they thought their donors would find most interesting, write a note in the margin, and mail it to them in an envelope.

A few weeks later, the legislative session started in the state capital. The WTA lobbyist jotted down some notes in an e-mail about what issues they'd be working on, and the board members forwarded that to their donors, with an invitation to contact the lobbyist directly if they had questions or wanted to participate in the process.

As the session ended, WTA was sponsoring a large trails festival with a national figure as keynote speaker. The board members invited their two donors to join the speaker for a casual drink at the end of the day.

The board members, feeling more comfortable with their donors at each turn, invited them to participate in a private trail project, where the executive staff, the board, and the major donors spent a day in the mountains working side by side. At the end of that successful day, the board members told us they now felt ready to ask their donors for a gift.

I asked why they felt like it was okay now, when they had been so resistant just a few months before. The obvious answer was that they now had a relationship with the donors: they knew why each one cared about the organization, and which aspect of it inspired them most. They knew a little more about each donor's capacity to give. And they knew that every contact with the donors throughout the year had been:

- mission-related (not a golf tournament or some fancy affair);

- authentic (not a manipulative ploy, but a genuine connection);

- timely (news was shared when it was new and relevant);

- cheap or free to implement (WTA wasn't spending money to build relationships with the donors); and

- value-added (the touch points were to meet the needs of the donors— not the organization—and the donors couldn't buy or have those experiences or opportunities anywhere else)

The most important thing was that the board members felt pretty certain that their donors would respond positively to them and to their request.

Now that they were ready, we showed the board members how to approach someone with a personal request, and sent them off to make their appointments. Within a month, they'd all met with their donors, had easy conversations that were an organic outgrowth of their relationships, and garnered gifts that totaled twice the value of the year before.

The group of donors that Washington Trails had stewarded that year became their major gifts "club," and contributions from that group generate about 90 percent of the contributed income for WTA each year.

The board members enjoyed the process because they felt like they were being given tasks that fit their comfort zones, their skill sets, their busy schedules, and their personal interests.

They also appreciated that the contact with the donors wasn't predictable: it varied from e-mail to voice mail, snail mail to in-person—whatever suited that particular touch point.

They noted especially that the process reflected a strategy that made sense—inner circle; top of the donor pyramid; renewal and upgrade, not acquisition; low-cost contact; relationship building before asking; and asking only when they knew the donors were ready.

But the most important lesson from the experience was that their job as board members was to *help donors have the relationship with the mission they were longing for*, but were unable to get through e-newsletters and big events. When they focused on the donors' authentic connections to the mission, fundraising became joyful.

Where Do We Start?

I trust you're already doing some of this well. Congratulate yourself and celebrate with the board.

If you saw some opportunities for improvement here, you're probably wondering how to squeeze them into a schedule that's already too full.

Hopefully some of the concepts in the strategy section will help you let go of some things that don't make sense any more, like focusing on new donors. But here are some other easy suggestions for getting started:

• Involve board members in thanking donors by having them sign cards, make calls, send e-mails or share stories of impact.

- Reshape your board meetings to feature more generative conversations and fewer reports.

- Invite the board to practice articulating your "so whats" and asking open-ended questions.

These activities will offer almost instant success—and leaders will be able to feel the difference.

> "Tug on anything at all and you'll find it connected to everything else in the universe."
> —JOHN MUIR

As you begin to address the barriers in these pages, you'll discover that each one is inextricably linked to the others. Because your organization is a system, your efforts to tackle one barrier will surely affect another. So it might just get easier as you go!

And remember that none of this is the responsibility of any one person or position: eliminating these barriers is a collective effort, involving both board and staff.

I hope that taking even one of the steps in these pages helps light a fire under your board members, who know in their hearts that good fundraising isn't about money—it's about finding people with a natural affinity for your mission and helping them connect to what gives them meaning.

If we help board members build genuine relationships between our donors and our mission, the money will follow. Good leaders know that. Just like they know that ripe fruit falls effortlessly into your hand when the time is right.

Let's invest in our board members so they embrace every aspect of their role with gusto. So they're on fire about the mission and goals, so they understand the context and the budget, so they're clear about what's expected of them and how they can best serve the organization. And let's give them the tools and support they need to connect authentically with donors.

Then watch them raise money joyfully.

Good luck!

Acknowledgments

The individuals who deserve my deepest thanks are the thousands of board members, executive directors and development directors with whom I learned these lessons over the past 35 years.

Elizabeth Lunney, former Executive Director of Washington Trails Association, and Lace Thornberg, the Development Director at the time, were willing and imaginative collaborators as we experimented with their board.

Sonya Campion proposed the deadline that motivated me to write down what I've been saying.

Good friends Eileen Allen (author of *I Love Being Old!*) and JoAnne Heron offered beautiful places for me to think and write.

Colleagues read early versions and offered gentle suggestions: Kathe Shaw-Bassett, Mary Gleason, Barbara Green, Tara Morgan and Zoë Myers.

Christopher and Stephanie Davenport (501 Videos), Sheila Hoffman (Hoffman Graphics) and Beth Sanders (videographer) augmented the book with their technological prowess. Karalynn Ott and Michele Whitehead (Verve Editorial) and Zach Hooker handled editing and design.

Kim Klein first inspired me at a board retreat in the 70s, demonstrating that when fundraising is connected to our deepest values, it's not only joyful—it can be a powerful tool for changing the world. Her amazing career has given me a soulful path to follow. And Penelope Burk has added new zest and rigor to our field in recent years.

My husband and fellow publisher, David Bauman, has shown me what deep joy can come from a relationship that is cultivated and stewarded, enlivened by generative conversations and focused on shared mission. Thank you!

About the Author

Susan Howlett has helped nonprofits raise money joyfully for 35 years, as a board member, a development director, an executive director, and—for the last 23 years — as a consultant to more than 1000 organizations across the U.S. She has worked with unstaffed organizations with tiny budgets and national organizations with multi-million dollar budgets; with grassroots groups and sophisticated mature institutions; in every field imaginable. She has been core faculty in the University of Washington's year-long Certificate Program in Fundraising Management for 20 years.

Co-author of the widely-used *Getting Funded: The Complete Guide to Writing Grant Proposals*, Susan is hired regularly by grantors to strengthen the nonprofits they fund. She has spent decades leading several professional associations, and served as a subject matter expert for the national Grant Professionals Certification Institute. And she's been a funder herself in several contexts.

A sought-after speaker, trainer, and mentor, Susan is known for engaging her audiences in joyful discovery with the liberal use of stories, humor, and chocolate.